# 50 Beginner-Friendly Cooking Recipes for Home

By: Kelly Johnson

# Table of Contents

- Grilled Chicken Salad
- Spaghetti Bolognese
- Vegetable Stir-Fry
- Classic Margherita Pizza
- Creamy Tomato Soup
- Baked Ziti
- Roasted Lemon Garlic Chicken
- Pancakes with Maple Syrup
- Beef Tacos
- Garlic Butter Shrimp
- Caprese Salad
- Chicken Alfredo Pasta
- Beef and Broccoli Stir-Fry
- Homemade Macaroni and Cheese
- Greek Salad
- Chicken Quesadillas
- Oven-Baked BBQ Chicken
- Mushroom Risotto
- Caesar Salad
- Vegetable Omelette
- Chili Con Carne
- Spinach and Feta Stuffed Chicken Breast
- Teriyaki Salmon
- Quinoa Salad
- Egg Fried Rice
- Roasted Vegetables
- Chicken Parmesan
- Shrimp Scampi
- Caprese Panini
- Sweet Potato Fries
- Beef Stroganoff
- Tomato Basil Bruschetta
- Chicken Fajitas
- One-Pot Chicken and Rice
- Broccoli Cheddar Soup

- Margherita Flatbread
- Creamy Garlic Mashed Potatoes
- Pesto Pasta
- Honey Garlic Glazed Salmon
- Avocado Toast
- Lemon Herb Roasted Potatoes
- Chicken Caesar Wraps
- Ratatouille
- Stuffed Bell Peppers
- Creamy Spinach Artichoke Dip
- Lemon Butter Tilapia
- Sausage and Peppers
- Chicken Noodle Soup
- BBQ Pulled Pork Sandwiches
- Chocolate Chip Cookies

**Grilled Chicken Salad**

Ingredients:

For the Grilled Chicken:

- 2 boneless, skinless chicken breasts
- 2 tablespoons olive oil
- 1 teaspoon dried oregano
- 1 teaspoon paprika
- Salt and pepper to taste

For the Salad:

- Mixed salad greens (lettuce, spinach, arugula, etc.)
- Cherry tomatoes, halved
- Cucumber, sliced
- Red onion, thinly sliced
- Avocado, sliced
- Feta cheese, crumbled

For the Dressing:

- 3 tablespoons olive oil
- 2 tablespoons balsamic vinegar
- 1 teaspoon Dijon mustard
- 1 clove garlic, minced
- Salt and pepper to taste

Instructions:

Preheat your grill or grill pan over medium-high heat.
In a small bowl, mix together the olive oil, dried oregano, paprika, salt, and pepper to create a marinade for the chicken.
Pat the chicken breasts dry with paper towels and brush them with the marinade on both sides.

Grill the chicken breasts for 6-8 minutes per side or until they reach an internal temperature of 165°F (74°C). Cooking times may vary depending on the thickness of the chicken breasts.

While the chicken is grilling, prepare the salad ingredients. Combine the mixed salad greens, cherry tomatoes, cucumber, red onion, avocado, and feta cheese in a large salad bowl.

In a separate small bowl, whisk together the olive oil, balsamic vinegar, Dijon mustard, minced garlic, salt, and pepper to create the dressing.

Once the chicken is cooked, let it rest for a few minutes before slicing it into thin strips.

Add the grilled chicken strips to the salad.

Drizzle the dressing over the salad and toss everything gently to combine.

Serve the grilled chicken salad immediately and enjoy your healthy and flavorful meal!

Feel free to customize the salad with your favorite vegetables and toppings. You can also add nuts or seeds for extra crunch. Enjoy!

**Spaghetti Bolognese**

Ingredients:

- 1 pound (450g) ground beef (you can also use a mix of beef and pork)
- 1 onion, finely chopped
- 2 cloves garlic, minced
- 1 carrot, finely chopped
- 1 celery stalk, finely chopped
- 1 can (14 ounces/400g) crushed tomatoes
- 2 tablespoons tomato paste
- 1/2 cup (120ml) red wine (optional)
- 1 teaspoon dried oregano
- 1 teaspoon dried basil
- Salt and pepper to taste
- Olive oil
- 1 pound (450g) spaghetti noodles
- Grated Parmesan cheese (optional), for serving

Instructions:

Heat a few tablespoons of olive oil in a large skillet or saucepan over medium heat.

Add the chopped onion, garlic, carrot, and celery. Sauté until the vegetables are softened and the onion is translucent.

Add the ground beef to the skillet, breaking it up with a spoon. Cook until the meat is browned and cooked through.

Stir in the tomato paste and cook for a couple of minutes to enhance its flavor.

Pour in the crushed tomatoes and red wine (if using). Add the dried oregano, basil, salt, and pepper. Stir well to combine.

Bring the sauce to a simmer, then reduce the heat to low. Cover the skillet and let the sauce simmer for at least 30 minutes to allow the flavors to meld. If you have more time, you can let it simmer for longer.

While the sauce is simmering, cook the spaghetti noodles according to the package instructions. Drain and set aside.

Once the sauce has thickened and developed its flavors, taste and adjust the seasonings if needed.

Serve the Bolognese sauce over the cooked spaghetti noodles. Optionally, sprinkle grated Parmesan cheese on top.

Enjoy your homemade Spaghetti Bolognese!

**Vegetable Stir-Fry**

Ingredients:

- 1 tablespoon vegetable oil (such as sesame oil or peanut oil)
- 1 onion, thinly sliced
- 2 cloves garlic, minced
- 1-inch piece of ginger, grated
- 1 bell pepper, thinly sliced (use a mix of colors for variety)
- 1 carrot, julienned or thinly sliced
- 1 zucchini, thinly sliced
- 1 cup broccoli florets
- 1 cup snap peas, trimmed
- 1 cup mushrooms, sliced
- 2 tablespoons soy sauce
- 1 tablespoon oyster sauce (optional)
- 1 tablespoon hoisin sauce (optional)
- 1 tablespoon rice vinegar
- 1 teaspoon sesame seeds (optional)
- Cooked rice or noodles for serving

Instructions:

Prepare the Vegetables:
- Wash, peel, and chop all the vegetables as needed.
- Keep them separate to add to the stir-fry at different times, considering their cooking times.

Heat the Wok or Skillet:
- Place a wok or large skillet over medium-high heat.
- Add the vegetable oil and let it heat for a moment.

Cook the Aromatics:
- Add the sliced onion, minced garlic, and grated ginger to the wok.
- Stir-fry for about 1-2 minutes until fragrant.

Stir-Fry the Vegetables:
- Start adding the vegetables with longer cooking times first, such as broccoli and carrots.
- Stir-fry for a few minutes until they begin to soften.

Add More Vegetables:

- Add the bell peppers, zucchini, snap peas, and mushrooms.
- Continue stir-frying for another 2-3 minutes until the vegetables are tender-crisp.

Sauce it Up:
- In a small bowl, mix soy sauce, oyster sauce (if using), hoisin sauce (if using), and rice vinegar.
- Pour the sauce over the vegetables in the wok and toss to coat evenly.

Finish and Serve:
- Continue cooking for an additional 1-2 minutes until the sauce thickens slightly.
- Sprinkle sesame seeds on top if desired.

Serve:
- Serve the vegetable stir-fry over cooked rice or noodles.

Feel free to experiment with different vegetables, sauces, and protein sources (such as tofu, chicken, or shrimp) to create your own customized vegetable stir-fry. Enjoy!

**Classic Margherita Pizza**

Ingredients:

For the Pizza Dough:

- 1 pound (about 4 cups) pizza dough (store-bought or homemade)
- Cornmeal or flour for dusting

For the Pizza Sauce:

- 1 can (14 ounces) crushed tomatoes
- 2 cloves garlic, minced
- 1 tablespoon olive oil
- Salt and pepper to taste
- 1 teaspoon dried oregano (optional)

For the Toppings:

- Fresh mozzarella cheese, sliced
- Fresh basil leaves
- Extra-virgin olive oil for drizzling

Instructions:

Preheat the Oven:
- Preheat your oven to the highest temperature it can go (usually around 475-500°F or 245-260°C). If you have a pizza stone, place it in the oven during preheating.

Prepare the Pizza Dough:
- If using store-bought dough, follow the package instructions for bringing it to room temperature.
- If making homemade dough, roll it out on a floured surface to your desired thickness.

Prepare the Pizza Sauce:
- In a bowl, mix together the crushed tomatoes, minced garlic, olive oil, salt, pepper, and dried oregano (if using).

Assemble the Pizza:
- If using a pizza stone, sprinkle it with cornmeal or flour. Alternatively, use a parchment paper-lined baking sheet.
- Place the rolled-out pizza dough on the prepared surface.
- Spread a thin layer of the pizza sauce over the dough, leaving a small border around the edges.
- Arrange slices of fresh mozzarella evenly over the sauce.

Bake the Pizza:
- If using a pizza stone, carefully transfer the pizza to the preheated stone in the oven. If using a baking sheet, place it directly in the oven.
- Bake for about 10-12 minutes or until the crust is golden and the cheese is melted and bubbly.

Add Fresh Basil:
- Remove the pizza from the oven and immediately scatter fresh basil leaves over the hot pizza.

Finish with Olive Oil:
- Drizzle extra-virgin olive oil over the top of the pizza for added flavor.

Slice and Serve:
- Allow the pizza to cool for a minute before slicing. Serve hot and enjoy your Classic Margherita Pizza!

Feel free to get creative and add your own twists to this classic recipe. It's a perfect canvas for customization.

**Creamy Tomato Soup**

Ingredients:

- 2 tablespoons butter
- 1 onion, chopped
- 2 cloves garlic, minced
- 1 can (28 ounces) crushed tomatoes
- 1 can (14 ounces) diced tomatoes
- 1 teaspoon sugar
- 1 teaspoon dried basil
- 1 teaspoon dried oregano
- 1/2 teaspoon salt (adjust to taste)
- 1/4 teaspoon black pepper
- 2 cups vegetable or chicken broth
- 1/2 cup heavy cream
- Fresh basil or parsley for garnish (optional)

Instructions:

Sauté Vegetables:
- In a large pot, melt the butter over medium heat. Add the chopped onion and cook until it becomes translucent.

Add Garlic and Tomatoes:
- Add the minced garlic to the pot and cook for about 1 minute until fragrant.
- Pour in both the crushed and diced tomatoes, including their juices.

Season and Simmer:
- Add sugar, dried basil, dried oregano, salt, and black pepper to the pot. Stir well.
- Pour in the vegetable or chicken broth and bring the mixture to a simmer. Allow it to simmer for about 15-20 minutes, allowing the flavors to meld.

Blend the Soup:
- Use an immersion blender to carefully blend the soup until smooth. Alternatively, transfer the soup in batches to a blender and blend until smooth. Be cautious when blending hot liquids.

Add Cream:

- Return the blended soup to the pot. Stir in the heavy cream and let it simmer for an additional 5 minutes.

Adjust Seasoning:
- Taste the soup and adjust the seasoning if needed, adding more salt or pepper according to your preference.

Serve:
- Ladle the creamy tomato soup into bowls. Garnish with fresh basil or parsley if desired.

Enjoy:
- Serve the creamy tomato soup hot, perhaps with a sprinkle of black pepper or a drizzle of cream on top. It pairs wonderfully with crusty bread or a grilled cheese sandwich.

This creamy tomato soup is a comforting classic, perfect for chilly days or whenever you're in the mood for a warm and satisfying meal.

**Baked Ziti**

Ingredients:

- 1 pound (16 ounces) ziti pasta
- 1 tablespoon olive oil
- 1 onion, finely chopped
- 2 cloves garlic, minced
- 1 pound ground beef or Italian sausage (optional)
- 1 can (28 ounces) crushed tomatoes
- 1 can (14 ounces) diced tomatoes
- 1 teaspoon dried oregano
- 1 teaspoon dried basil
- Salt and pepper to taste
- 1/2 cup grated Parmesan cheese
- 2 cups ricotta cheese
- 2 cups shredded mozzarella cheese
- Fresh basil or parsley for garnish (optional)

Instructions:

Preheat the Oven:
- Preheat your oven to 375°F (190°C).

Cook the Ziti:
- Cook the ziti pasta according to the package instructions until just al dente. Drain and set aside.

Prepare the Sauce:
- In a large skillet, heat olive oil over medium heat. Add chopped onions and garlic, and sauté until softened.
- If using ground beef or sausage, add it to the skillet and cook until browned. Drain excess fat.
- Stir in crushed tomatoes, diced tomatoes, dried oregano, dried basil, salt, and pepper. Simmer for about 15-20 minutes, allowing the flavors to meld.

Combine Pasta and Sauce:
- Add the cooked ziti pasta to the sauce, tossing to coat the pasta evenly.

Layering:
- In a large baking dish, spread half of the ziti and sauce mixture evenly.
- Dollop half of the ricotta cheese over the pasta and sauce. Sprinkle with half of the mozzarella and Parmesan.

Repeat Layers:
- Repeat the layering with the remaining ziti, sauce, ricotta, mozzarella, and Parmesan.

Bake:
- Cover the baking dish with aluminum foil and bake in the preheated oven for 25-30 minutes. Then, remove the foil and bake for an additional 10-15 minutes until the cheese is melted and bubbly, and the edges are golden.

Serve:
- Allow the Baked Ziti to cool for a few minutes before serving. Garnish with fresh basil or parsley if desired.

Baked Ziti is a crowd-pleaser and a great dish for gatherings. Serve it with a side of garlic bread or a simple salad for a complete and satisfying meal.

**Roasted Lemon Garlic Chicken**

Ingredients:

- 1 whole chicken (about 4-5 pounds)
- 2 lemons, sliced
- 1 head of garlic, halved horizontally
- 2 tablespoons olive oil
- 2 teaspoons dried thyme
- 1 teaspoon dried rosemary
- Salt and black pepper to taste
- 1 cup chicken broth or water
- Fresh herbs (such as parsley or thyme) for garnish (optional)

Instructions:

Preheat the Oven:
- Preheat your oven to 425°F (220°C).

Prepare the Chicken:
- Rinse the whole chicken inside and out under cold running water. Pat it dry with paper towels.
- Season the chicken cavity with salt and pepper.
- Place lemon slices and garlic halves inside the cavity.

Season the Chicken:
- In a small bowl, mix olive oil, dried thyme, dried rosemary, salt, and black pepper to create a herb-infused oil.
- Rub the outside of the chicken with the herb-infused oil, ensuring it's evenly coated.

Tie the Legs:
- If your chicken comes with the legs untied, tie them together with kitchen twine to help the chicken cook evenly.

Roasting Pan:
- Place the chicken in a roasting pan or a baking dish with a rack.

Roast the Chicken:
- Roast the chicken in the preheated oven for about 1 hour and 15 minutes to 1 hour and 30 minutes, or until the internal temperature reaches 165°F (74°C). The skin should be golden and crispy.

Baste the Chicken:

- Every 30 minutes, baste the chicken with pan juices to keep it moist. If the skin is getting too brown, you can cover it with foil.

Rest the Chicken:
- Once the chicken is cooked, remove it from the oven and let it rest for about 10-15 minutes before carving.

Make Gravy (Optional):
- If you want to make a simple gravy, place the roasting pan on the stovetop over medium heat. Add chicken broth or water and scrape up any browned bits from the bottom. Simmer until it thickens slightly.

Serve:
- Carve the roasted lemon garlic chicken, garnish with fresh herbs if desired, and serve with the optional gravy.

Enjoy your flavorful and juicy Roasted Lemon Garlic Chicken! This dish pairs well with roasted vegetables, mashed potatoes, or a side salad.

**Pancakes with Maple Syrup**

Ingredients:

- 1 cup all-purpose flour
- 2 tablespoons granulated sugar
- 1 teaspoon baking powder
- 1/2 teaspoon baking soda
- 1/4 teaspoon salt
- 3/4 cup buttermilk
- 1/4 cup milk
- 1 large egg
- 2 tablespoons unsalted butter, melted
- Cooking spray or additional butter for greasing the pan
- Pure maple syrup for serving

Instructions:

Preheat the Griddle or Pan:
- Preheat a griddle or a non-stick skillet over medium heat. If using a griddle, set it to 350°F (175°C).

Prepare the Dry Ingredients:
- In a large mixing bowl, whisk together the flour, sugar, baking powder, baking soda, and salt.

Combine Wet Ingredients:
- In another bowl, whisk together the buttermilk, milk, egg, and melted butter.

Combine Wet and Dry Ingredients:
- Pour the wet ingredients into the dry ingredients and gently stir until just combined. It's okay if there are a few lumps.

Cook the Pancakes:
- Lightly grease the griddle or skillet with cooking spray or a small amount of butter.
- Pour 1/4 cup portions of batter onto the hot griddle for each pancake, leaving space between them.
- Cook until bubbles form on the surface of the pancakes and the edges start to look set, about 2-3 minutes.

Flip and Cook the Other Side:

- Carefully flip each pancake with a spatula and cook for an additional 1-2 minutes on the other side, or until golden brown.

Keep Warm:
- Transfer the cooked pancakes to a plate and cover with a kitchen towel to keep them warm while you cook the remaining batter.

Serve with Maple Syrup:
- Stack the pancakes on serving plates and drizzle with pure maple syrup.

Optional Toppings:
- Customize your pancakes by adding toppings such as sliced fruits, whipped cream, or chopped nuts if desired.

Enjoy your delicious and fluffy pancakes with maple syrup! This classic breakfast is sure to be a crowd-pleaser.

**Beef Tacos**

Ingredients:

For the Beef Filling:

- 1 pound ground beef
- 1 small onion, finely chopped
- 2 cloves garlic, minced
- 1 tablespoon chili powder
- 1 teaspoon ground cumin
- 1/2 teaspoon paprika
- 1/2 teaspoon dried oregano
- Salt and pepper to taste
- 1/2 cup beef broth or water

For Assembling Tacos:

- Hard or soft taco shells
- Shredded lettuce
- Diced tomatoes
- Shredded cheese (cheddar or Mexican blend)
- Sour cream
- Salsa or pico de gallo
- Sliced jalapeños (optional)
- Fresh cilantro, chopped (optional)
- Lime wedges

Instructions:

Cook the Beef Filling:
- In a large skillet over medium-high heat, cook the ground beef, breaking it apart with a spoon, until browned and cooked through.
- Drain any excess fat from the skillet.
- Add chopped onions and minced garlic to the beef, cooking until the onions are softened.

Season the Beef:

- Sprinkle chili powder, ground cumin, paprika, dried oregano, salt, and pepper over the beef mixture.
- Stir well to evenly distribute the spices.

Add Liquid:
- Pour in beef broth or water, stirring to combine. Allow the mixture to simmer for 5-7 minutes until the liquid reduces and flavors meld.

Prepare Taco Shells:
- If using hard taco shells, follow the package instructions to heat them in the oven.
- If using soft tortillas, warm them in a dry skillet or microwave according to the package instructions.

Assemble Tacos:
- Spoon the seasoned beef mixture into each taco shell.
- Top with shredded lettuce, diced tomatoes, shredded cheese, sour cream, salsa, and any other desired toppings.

Garnish and Serve:
- Garnish with sliced jalapeños, fresh cilantro, and lime wedges if desired.
- Serve the beef tacos immediately while warm.

Enjoy:
- Customize your beef tacos with your favorite toppings and enjoy a delicious and satisfying meal.

Feel free to get creative with your taco toppings and adjust the seasoning to your taste.

Beef tacos are perfect for a quick and flavorful weeknight dinner or for entertaining guests.

**Garlic Butter Shrimp**

Ingredients:

- 1 pound large shrimp, peeled and deveined
- Salt and black pepper to taste
- 3 tablespoons unsalted butter
- 4 cloves garlic, minced
- 1/2 teaspoon red pepper flakes (optional, for a bit of heat)
- 1 tablespoon lemon juice
- 2 tablespoons fresh parsley, chopped
- Lemon wedges for serving

Instructions:

Prepare the Shrimp:
- Pat the shrimp dry with paper towels and season with salt and black pepper.

Heat the Butter:
- In a large skillet, melt the butter over medium heat.

Cook the Shrimp:
- Add the minced garlic and red pepper flakes (if using) to the melted butter. Sauté for about 1 minute until the garlic is fragrant.
- Add the seasoned shrimp to the skillet in a single layer. Cook for 1-2 minutes per side, or until the shrimp turns pink and opaque. Be careful not to overcook, as shrimp can become rubbery.

Add Lemon Juice:
- Squeeze lemon juice over the cooked shrimp and stir to combine. This adds a bright and fresh flavor to the dish.

Garnish:
- Sprinkle chopped fresh parsley over the shrimp. The parsley adds color and freshness to the dish.

Serve:
- Transfer the garlic butter shrimp to a serving platter.
- Serve immediately, garnished with additional chopped parsley and lemon wedges on the side.

Optional Serving Suggestions:
- Enjoy the garlic butter shrimp over cooked pasta, rice, or with a side of crusty bread to soak up the flavorful sauce.

Enjoy:
- Serve this quick and flavorful garlic butter shrimp as a main dish or as part of a seafood feast.

Feel free to customize the recipe by adding your favorite herbs or adjusting the level of spiciness. This dish is versatile and pairs well with various side dishes to suit your preferences.

**Caprese Salad**

Ingredients:

- 4 large ripe tomatoes, sliced
- 1 pound fresh mozzarella cheese, sliced
- Fresh basil leaves
- Extra-virgin olive oil
- Balsamic glaze (optional)
- Salt and pepper to taste

Instructions:

Slice Tomatoes and Mozzarella:
- Wash and slice the tomatoes and mozzarella into rounds, approximately 1/4 inch thick.

Assemble the Salad:
- Arrange the tomato and mozzarella slices on a serving platter, alternating them or layering them in a circular pattern.

Add Basil Leaves:
- Tuck fresh basil leaves between the tomato and mozzarella slices. You can use whole leaves or chiffonade (thinly sliced) basil, depending on your preference.

Drizzle with Olive Oil:
- Drizzle extra-virgin olive oil over the tomato and mozzarella slices. Use a good quality olive oil for the best flavor.

Season with Salt and Pepper:
- Sprinkle salt and pepper over the salad to taste. Keep in mind that the mozzarella can be a bit salty, so you may not need much salt.

Optional Balsamic Glaze:
- Optionally, you can drizzle a balsamic glaze over the salad for added sweetness and acidity. This step is entirely optional, and traditional Caprese salads often skip this.

Serve:
- Serve the Caprese salad immediately, allowing the flavors to shine at room temperature.

Enjoy:

- Enjoy this simple and elegant Caprese salad as a light and refreshing appetizer or side dish.

Caprese salad is at its best when made with high-quality, fresh ingredients. It's a perfect dish to showcase the beauty of summer tomatoes and the combination of flavors that make Italian cuisine so beloved.

**Chicken Alfredo Pasta**

Ingredients:

- 8 ounces (about 225g) fettuccine pasta
- 1 pound (about 450g) boneless, skinless chicken breasts, cut into bite-sized pieces
- Salt and black pepper to taste
- 2 tablespoons olive oil
- 4 cloves garlic, minced
- 1 cup heavy cream
- 1 cup grated Parmesan cheese
- 1/2 cup unsalted butter
- 1/2 cup grated mozzarella cheese (optional)
- Fresh parsley, chopped, for garnish (optional)

Instructions:

Cook the Pasta:
- Cook the fettuccine pasta according to the package instructions in a large pot of salted boiling water until al dente. Drain and set aside.

Season and Cook the Chicken:
- Season the chicken pieces with salt and black pepper.
- In a large skillet, heat olive oil over medium-high heat. Add the seasoned chicken and cook until browned and cooked through. Remove the cooked chicken from the skillet and set aside.

Prepare the Alfredo Sauce:
- In the same skillet, add minced garlic and sauté for about 1 minute until fragrant.
- Reduce the heat to medium-low and add the heavy cream, Parmesan cheese, and butter to the skillet. Stir continuously until the cheese is melted and the sauce is smooth and creamy.

Combine Chicken and Sauce:
- Return the cooked chicken to the skillet with the Alfredo sauce. Add the drained fettuccine pasta and toss everything together until well-coated in the sauce.

Optional Cheese Topping:

- If desired, sprinkle grated mozzarella cheese over the top of the pasta and chicken mixture. Cover the skillet with a lid and let it melt for a few minutes until bubbly.

Garnish and Serve:
- Garnish with chopped fresh parsley if desired.
- Serve the Chicken Alfredo Pasta hot, and enjoy this comforting and satisfying dish.

Chicken Alfredo pasta is a crowd-pleaser and perfect for a cozy dinner. You can also customize the recipe by adding vegetables like broccoli or spinach for extra flavor and nutrition.

**Beef and Broccoli Stir-Fry**

Ingredients:

For the Beef Marinade:

- 1 pound (about 450g) flank steak or sirloin, thinly sliced
- 2 tablespoons soy sauce
- 1 tablespoon oyster sauce
- 1 tablespoon cornstarch
- 1 teaspoon sesame oil
- 1 teaspoon sugar
- 1/2 teaspoon black pepper

For the Stir-Fry Sauce:

- 1/4 cup soy sauce
- 2 tablespoons oyster sauce
- 1 tablespoon hoisin sauce
- 2 teaspoons cornstarch
- 1 teaspoon sugar
- 1/2 cup beef broth or water

Other Ingredients:

- 2 tablespoons vegetable oil (for cooking)
- 3 cups broccoli florets
- 2 cloves garlic, minced
- 1 teaspoon fresh ginger, grated
- Cooked rice for serving

Instructions:

Marinate the Beef:
- In a bowl, combine the sliced beef with soy sauce, oyster sauce, cornstarch, sesame oil, sugar, and black pepper. Let it marinate for at least 15-20 minutes.

Prepare the Stir-Fry Sauce:
- In a separate bowl, whisk together soy sauce, oyster sauce, hoisin sauce, cornstarch, sugar, and beef broth (or water). Set aside.

Cook the Broccoli:
- Blanch the broccoli in boiling water for about 2 minutes until it becomes bright green and slightly tender. Drain and set aside.

Stir-Fry the Beef:
- Heat vegetable oil in a wok or large skillet over high heat.
- Add the marinated beef and stir-fry for 2-3 minutes until browned and cooked through. Remove the beef from the wok and set aside.

Stir-Fry Aromatics:
- In the same wok, add a bit more oil if needed. Add minced garlic and grated ginger, and stir-fry for about 30 seconds until fragrant.

Combine Beef, Broccoli, and Sauce:
- Return the cooked beef to the wok, add the blanched broccoli, and pour in the prepared stir-fry sauce. Toss everything together until well-coated and heated through.

Finish and Serve:
- Continue stir-frying for an additional 1-2 minutes until the sauce thickens.
- Serve the Beef and Broccoli Stir-Fry over cooked rice.

Garnish (Optional):
- Garnish with sesame seeds or chopped green onions if desired.

Enjoy your homemade Beef and Broccoli Stir-Fry, a delicious and satisfying dish that's ready in no time!

**Homemade Macaroni and Cheese**

Ingredients:

- 8 ounces (about 2 cups) elbow macaroni or any pasta shape you prefer
- 1/4 cup unsalted butter
- 1/4 cup all-purpose flour
- 1/2 teaspoon salt
- 1/4 teaspoon black pepper
- 1/4 teaspoon mustard powder (optional)
- 2 cups milk
- 2 1/2 cups shredded sharp cheddar cheese
- 1/2 cup shredded mozzarella cheese (optional, for extra creaminess)
- 1/2 cup breadcrumbs (optional, for topping)

Instructions:

Cook the Macaroni:
- Cook the macaroni according to the package instructions in a large pot of salted boiling water until al dente. Drain and set aside.

Make the Cheese Sauce:
- In a saucepan over medium heat, melt the butter.
- Add flour, salt, black pepper, and mustard powder (if using). Stir continuously to create a roux, cooking for 1-2 minutes until it becomes a light golden color.

Add Milk:
- Gradually whisk in the milk to the roux, ensuring there are no lumps. Continue cooking and stirring until the mixture thickens, about 5-7 minutes.

Melt Cheese:
- Reduce the heat to low, then add the shredded cheddar cheese (and mozzarella if using), stirring until the cheese is completely melted and the sauce is smooth.

Combine Sauce and Pasta:
- Add the cooked macaroni to the cheese sauce, stirring to coat the pasta evenly.

Optional Breadcrumb Topping:

- If you want a breadcrumb topping, melt a tablespoon of butter in a small skillet. Add breadcrumbs and toast until golden brown.

Bake (Optional):
- Preheat your oven to 350°F (175°C). Transfer the macaroni and cheese to a baking dish. Sprinkle the breadcrumb topping over the top. Bake for 15-20 minutes until bubbly and golden.

Serve:
- Serve the macaroni and cheese hot, straight from the stovetop or after baking.

Enjoy your homemade macaroni and cheese! It's a versatile dish, and you can customize it by adding cooked bacon, sautéed onions, or other favorite mix-ins.

**Greek Salad**

Ingredients:

For the Salad:

- 4 medium tomatoes, chopped
- 1 cucumber, peeled and diced
- 1 red onion, thinly sliced
- 1 bell pepper (red, yellow, or green), chopped
- 1 cup Kalamata olives, pitted
- 1 cup feta cheese, crumbled
- 1 cup cherry tomatoes, halved
- 1/2 cup fresh parsley, chopped
- 1/2 cup fresh mint, chopped (optional)
- Salt and black pepper to taste

For the Dressing:

- 1/3 cup extra-virgin olive oil
- 2 tablespoons red wine vinegar
- 1 teaspoon dried oregano
- 1 clove garlic, minced
- Salt and black pepper to taste

Instructions:

Prepare the Vegetables:
- In a large salad bowl, combine chopped tomatoes, diced cucumber, sliced red onion, chopped bell pepper, Kalamata olives, cherry tomatoes, fresh parsley, and mint (if using).

Add Feta Cheese:
- Crumble the feta cheese over the top of the vegetables.

Season with Salt and Pepper:
- Season the salad with salt and black pepper to taste.

Make the Dressing:

- In a small bowl or jar, whisk together extra-virgin olive oil, red wine vinegar, dried oregano, minced garlic, salt, and black pepper. Adjust the seasoning to your taste.

Dress the Salad:
- Pour the dressing over the salad. Toss gently to combine, ensuring all the vegetables are coated with the dressing.

Serve:
- Let the Greek salad sit for a few minutes to allow the flavors to meld.
- Serve the salad in individual bowls or on a platter.

Garnish:
- Garnish with additional fresh herbs and extra feta cheese if desired.

Greek salad is a wonderful side dish or a light meal on its own. It's best enjoyed fresh, so serve it immediately or refrigerate until ready to serve. Pair it with crusty bread or grilled chicken for a more substantial meal.

**Chicken Quesadillas**

Ingredients:

- 2 cups cooked chicken, shredded or diced
- 1 cup shredded cheese (cheddar, Monterey Jack, or a Mexican blend)
- 1/2 cup diced bell peppers (any color)
- 1/4 cup diced red onion
- 1/4 cup chopped fresh cilantro (optional)
- 1 teaspoon ground cumin
- 1 teaspoon chili powder
- Salt and pepper to taste
- 4 large flour tortillas
- Cooking spray or a bit of vegetable oil for cooking
- Salsa, guacamole, or sour cream for serving (optional)

Instructions:

Prepare the Chicken:
- Season the cooked chicken with ground cumin, chili powder, salt, and pepper. Shred or dice it into bite-sized pieces.

Assemble the Quesadillas:
- Lay out the flour tortillas on a clean surface.
- Sprinkle a portion of shredded cheese evenly over half of each tortilla.
- Distribute the seasoned chicken, diced bell peppers, red onion, and chopped cilantro (if using) over the cheese.

Fold the Quesadillas:
- Fold the tortillas in half over the filling, creating a half-moon shape.

Cook the Quesadillas:
- Heat a large skillet or griddle over medium heat. If using a skillet, you may need to cook the quesadillas one at a time.
- Lightly coat the skillet with cooking spray or a small amount of vegetable oil.
- Place the filled and folded quesadilla onto the skillet and cook for 2-3 minutes on each side or until the tortilla becomes golden brown, and the cheese is melted.

Repeat:
- Repeat the process for the remaining quesadillas.

Slice and Serve:

- Once cooked, remove the quesadillas from the skillet and let them rest for a minute before slicing them into wedges.

Serve with Accompaniments:
- Serve the chicken quesadillas with your favorite accompaniments, such as salsa, guacamole, or sour cream.

Chicken quesadillas are versatile, and you can customize them by adding ingredients like black beans, corn, or jalapeños to suit your taste. Enjoy this quick and tasty Mexican-inspired dish!

**Oven-Baked BBQ Chicken**

Ingredients:

- 4-6 bone-in, skin-on chicken pieces (such as thighs, drumsticks, or a combination)
- Salt and black pepper to taste
- 1 teaspoon garlic powder
- 1 teaspoon onion powder
- 1 teaspoon paprika
- 1/2 teaspoon cayenne pepper (optional, for added heat)
- 1 cup barbecue sauce (store-bought or homemade)
- 2 tablespoons olive oil
- Fresh parsley or chopped green onions for garnish (optional)

Instructions:

Preheat the Oven:
- Preheat your oven to 400°F (200°C).

Prepare the Chicken:
- Pat the chicken pieces dry with paper towels. Season them with salt, black pepper, garlic powder, onion powder, paprika, and cayenne pepper (if using). Ensure the chicken is evenly coated with the seasoning.

Preheat a Skillet:
- Heat olive oil in an oven-safe skillet or a cast-iron pan over medium-high heat.

Sear the Chicken:
- Place the chicken pieces skin-side down in the hot skillet and sear for 3-4 minutes until the skin is golden brown. Flip and sear the other side for an additional 3-4 minutes.

Apply BBQ Sauce:
- Brush each chicken piece with barbecue sauce, ensuring they are well-coated.

Transfer to Oven:
- Transfer the skillet to the preheated oven.

Bake:
- Bake the chicken in the oven for 25-30 minutes or until the internal temperature reaches 165°F (74°C) and the chicken is cooked through.

Baste and Broil (Optional):
- If you prefer a crispier skin, you can baste the chicken with additional barbecue sauce and broil for an additional 2-3 minutes until the skin is caramelized.

Garnish and Serve:
- Remove the skillet from the oven, and let the chicken rest for a few minutes.
- Garnish with fresh parsley or chopped green onions if desired.

Enjoy:
- Serve the oven-baked BBQ chicken hot, and enjoy this flavorful and easy dish!

This oven-baked BBQ chicken is great on its own or paired with your favorite side dishes like coleslaw, baked beans, or cornbread.

**Mushroom Risotto**

Ingredients:

- 1 1/2 cups Arborio rice
- 1/2 cup dry white wine
- 6 cups chicken or vegetable broth, kept warm
- 2 tablespoons olive oil
- 1 onion, finely chopped
- 2 cloves garlic, minced
- 8 ounces (about 225g) mushrooms (such as cremini or shiitake), sliced
- 1/2 cup grated Parmesan cheese
- Salt and black pepper to taste
- 2 tablespoons unsalted butter
- Fresh parsley, chopped, for garnish (optional)

Instructions:

Prepare the Broth:
- Warm the chicken or vegetable broth in a saucepan over low heat. Keep it warm throughout the cooking process.

Sauté Mushrooms:
- In a large skillet or wide pan, heat olive oil over medium heat. Add the chopped onion and sauté until softened, about 3-4 minutes.
- Add the minced garlic and sliced mushrooms to the skillet. Cook for another 5-7 minutes until the mushrooms are browned and have released their moisture.

Toast the Rice:
- Add Arborio rice to the skillet and cook, stirring, for 2-3 minutes until the rice is lightly toasted.

Deglaze with Wine:
- Pour the white wine into the skillet, stirring constantly until most of the liquid is absorbed.

Add Broth:
- Begin adding the warm broth, one ladle at a time, to the rice. Stir frequently and allow the liquid to be absorbed before adding the next ladle of broth. Continue this process until the rice is creamy and cooked al dente, about 18-20 minutes.

Season and Finish:

- Season the risotto with salt and black pepper to taste. Stir in grated Parmesan cheese and unsalted butter, ensuring a creamy consistency.

Garnish and Serve:
- Garnish the mushroom risotto with chopped fresh parsley if desired.
- Serve the risotto immediately while it's hot.

Mushroom risotto is a comforting and elegant dish that can be served as a main course or as a side dish. Enjoy its creamy texture and rich mushroom flavor!

**Caesar Salad**

Ingredients:

For the Caesar Dressing:

- 1/2 cup mayonnaise
- 2 tablespoons grated Parmesan cheese
- 1 tablespoon Dijon mustard
- 2 cloves garlic, minced
- 2 tablespoons fresh lemon juice
- 1 teaspoon Worcestershire sauce
- Salt and black pepper to taste
- 1/4 cup olive oil

For the Salad:

- 1 large head of romaine lettuce, washed and chopped
- 1 cup croutons (store-bought or homemade)
- 1/2 cup grated Parmesan cheese
- Lemon wedges for serving (optional)
- Anchovy fillets for garnish (optional)

Instructions:

Prepare the Dressing:
- In a bowl, whisk together mayonnaise, grated Parmesan cheese, Dijon mustard, minced garlic, fresh lemon juice, Worcestershire sauce, salt, and black pepper.
- Slowly drizzle in the olive oil while continuing to whisk, creating a smooth and creamy dressing.

Assemble the Salad:
- In a large salad bowl, toss the chopped romaine lettuce with the Caesar dressing until the leaves are well coated.

Add Croutons and Cheese:
- Add croutons and grated Parmesan cheese to the salad. Toss gently to combine.

Serve:
- Divide the Caesar salad among individual plates.

Garnish (Optional):
- Garnish with additional grated Parmesan cheese and anchovy fillets if desired.

Serve with Lemon Wedges:
- Serve the Caesar salad with lemon wedges on the side for an extra burst of citrus flavor.

Enjoy:
- Enjoy your homemade Caesar salad as a refreshing and classic side dish or add grilled chicken or shrimp for a complete meal.

Feel free to customize your Caesar salad by adding protein like grilled chicken or shrimp, or by including other ingredients like cherry tomatoes or avocado slices. This timeless salad is versatile and always a crowd-pleaser.

**Vegetable Omelette**

Ingredients:

- 3 large eggs
- Salt and black pepper to taste
- 1 tablespoon butter or cooking oil
- 1/4 cup bell peppers, diced (any color)
- 1/4 cup onions, diced
- 1/4 cup tomatoes, diced
- 1/4 cup mushrooms, sliced
- 1/4 cup spinach, chopped
- 1/4 cup shredded cheese (cheddar, feta, or your choice)
- Fresh herbs (such as parsley or chives) for garnish (optional)
- Salsa or hot sauce for serving (optional)

Instructions:

Prep Vegetables:
- Dice the bell peppers, onions, and tomatoes. Slice the mushrooms, and chop the spinach.

Whisk Eggs:
- In a bowl, whisk the eggs until well beaten. Season with salt and black pepper.

Sauté Vegetables:
- Heat butter or cooking oil in a non-stick skillet over medium heat.
- Add the diced bell peppers, onions, and mushrooms. Sauté for 2-3 minutes until the vegetables are softened.

Add Spinach and Tomatoes:
- Add chopped spinach and diced tomatoes to the skillet. Cook for an additional 1-2 minutes until the spinach wilts and the tomatoes soften.

Pour in Beaten Eggs:
- Pour the beaten eggs over the sautéed vegetables, ensuring they are evenly distributed.

Swirl and Cook:
- Swirl the skillet to spread the eggs evenly. Let the omelette cook undisturbed for a minute or two.

Add Cheese:

- Sprinkle shredded cheese over one half of the omelette.

Fold and Serve:
- Once the edges of the omelette start to set, carefully fold it in half using a spatula.

Garnish and Serve:
- Garnish with fresh herbs if desired.
- Slide the vegetable omelette onto a plate and serve hot.
- Optional: Serve with salsa or hot sauce on the side.

Enjoy:
- Enjoy your vegetable omelette as a wholesome and customizable breakfast or brunch option.

Feel free to experiment with different vegetables, cheeses, and herbs to create your favorite version of a vegetable omelette. It's a versatile dish that can be tailored to suit your taste preferences.

**Chili Con Carne**

Ingredients:

- 1 pound (about 450g) ground beef (or a mix of beef and pork)
- 1 large onion, chopped
- 3 cloves garlic, minced
- 1 bell pepper, chopped
- 1-2 jalapeño peppers, finely chopped (optional, for heat)
- 1 can (15 ounces) kidney beans, drained and rinsed
- 1 can (15 ounces) black beans, drained and rinsed
- 1 can (15 ounces) diced tomatoes
- 1 can (6 ounces) tomato paste
- 2 cups beef broth
- 2 tablespoons chili powder
- 1 tablespoon ground cumin
- 1 teaspoon paprika
- 1 teaspoon oregano
- 1/2 teaspoon cayenne pepper (optional, for extra heat)
- Salt and black pepper to taste
- Olive oil for cooking
- Toppings: shredded cheese, sour cream, chopped green onions, cilantro, etc.

Instructions:

Sauté Aromatics:
- In a large pot or Dutch oven, heat olive oil over medium heat. Add chopped onions and cook until softened, about 3-5 minutes.

Cook Ground Meat:
- Add minced garlic and cook for an additional 1-2 minutes until fragrant.
- Add ground beef (or beef and pork mix) to the pot. Cook until browned, breaking it apart with a spoon.

Add Spices:
- Sprinkle chili powder, ground cumin, paprika, oregano, and cayenne pepper (if using) over the browned meat. Stir well to coat the meat in the spices.

Combine Tomatoes and Beans:
- Add diced tomatoes, tomato paste, drained kidney beans, drained black beans, and chopped bell pepper to the pot. Stir to combine.

Pour in Beef Broth:
- Pour beef broth into the pot, stirring to incorporate all the ingredients.

Simmer:
- Bring the chili to a simmer. Reduce the heat to low, cover, and let it simmer for at least 30 minutes to allow the flavors to meld. Stir occasionally.

Season and Adjust:
- Taste the chili and season with salt and black pepper according to your preference. If you prefer more heat, you can add extra chili powder or cayenne pepper.

Serve:
- Ladle the chili into bowls and serve hot.
- Optional: Top with shredded cheese, a dollop of sour cream, chopped green onions, cilantro, or your favorite chili toppings.

Enjoy:
- Enjoy this hearty and flavorful chili con carne on its own or over rice, pasta, or a baked potato.

Chili con carne is a versatile dish, and you can customize it to suit your taste preferences. It's perfect for feeding a crowd or for warming up on a cold day.

**Spinach and Feta Stuffed Chicken Breast**

Ingredients:

- 4 boneless, skinless chicken breasts
- Salt and black pepper to taste
- 1 tablespoon olive oil
- 2 cloves garlic, minced
- 4 cups fresh spinach, chopped
- 1/2 cup feta cheese, crumbled
- 1/4 cup grated Parmesan cheese
- 1/2 teaspoon dried oregano
- 1/2 teaspoon dried thyme
- 1/2 teaspoon dried basil
- 1/4 teaspoon red pepper flakes (optional, for a bit of heat)
- Toothpicks or kitchen twine (to secure the chicken)
- Lemon wedges for serving (optional)

Instructions:

Preheat the Oven:
- Preheat your oven to 375°F (190°C).

Prepare the Chicken:
- Lay each chicken breast flat on a cutting board. Carefully slice a pocket into the side of each chicken breast, being careful not to cut all the way through.

Season Chicken:
- Season the inside and outside of each chicken breast with salt and black pepper.

Sauté Spinach and Garlic:
- In a skillet, heat olive oil over medium heat. Add minced garlic and sauté for about 30 seconds until fragrant.
- Add chopped spinach to the skillet and cook until wilted. Remove from heat.

Prepare Filling:
- In a bowl, combine the sautéed spinach and garlic with crumbled feta cheese, grated Parmesan cheese, dried oregano, dried thyme, dried basil, and red pepper flakes if using. Mix well.

Stuff Chicken:
- Spoon the spinach and feta mixture into the pockets of each chicken breast.

Secure with Toothpicks or Twine:
- If needed, secure the opening of each chicken breast with toothpicks or tie with kitchen twine to keep the stuffing inside.

Sear Chicken:
- In an oven-safe skillet, heat a bit more olive oil over medium-high heat. Sear the stuffed chicken breasts for 2-3 minutes on each side until golden brown.

Finish in the Oven:
- Transfer the skillet to the preheated oven and bake for about 20-25 minutes or until the chicken is cooked through and reaches an internal temperature of 165°F (74°C).

Serve:
- Remove toothpicks or twine before serving.
- Serve the spinach and feta stuffed chicken breasts hot, optionally with lemon wedges on the side.

This dish pairs well with a side of roasted vegetables, rice, or a fresh green salad. Enjoy your flavorful and satisfying spinach and feta stuffed chicken!

**Teriyaki Salmon**

Ingredients:

- 4 salmon fillets (about 6 ounces each), skin-on or skinless
- Salt and black pepper to taste
- 2 tablespoons vegetable oil (for searing)
- Sesame seeds and chopped green onions for garnish (optional)

For the Teriyaki Sauce:

- 1/3 cup soy sauce
- 3 tablespoons mirin (sweet rice wine)
- 2 tablespoons sake (or white wine)
- 2 tablespoons brown sugar
- 1 teaspoon fresh ginger, grated
- 1 teaspoon garlic, minced
- 1 teaspoon cornstarch (optional, for thickening)

Instructions:

Prepare the Teriyaki Sauce:
- In a small saucepan, combine soy sauce, mirin, sake, brown sugar, grated ginger, and minced garlic. Bring the mixture to a simmer over medium heat.

Thicken Sauce (Optional):
- If you prefer a thicker sauce, mix cornstarch with a small amount of water to create a slurry. Add the slurry to the simmering sauce and whisk continuously until it thickens. Remove from heat.

Season Salmon:
- Season the salmon fillets with salt and black pepper on both sides.

Sear Salmon:
- In a large skillet or non-stick pan, heat vegetable oil over medium-high heat. Place the salmon fillets in the pan, skin side down if they have skin. Sear for 3-4 minutes until the bottom is golden brown.

Flip and Cook:
- Carefully flip the salmon fillets using a spatula. Cook for an additional 2-3 minutes until the salmon is cooked to your desired doneness.

Glaze with Teriyaki Sauce:
- Pour the prepared teriyaki sauce over the salmon fillets, coating them evenly. Allow the sauce to simmer and glaze the salmon for another 1-2 minutes.

Serve:
- Transfer the teriyaki-glazed salmon fillets to serving plates.
- Optional: Garnish with sesame seeds and chopped green onions.

Enjoy:
- Serve the teriyaki salmon hot, paired with steamed rice or your favorite side dishes.

Teriyaki salmon is a quick and satisfying dish that brings together the delicate flavor of salmon with the sweet and savory notes of teriyaki sauce. It's a versatile recipe that's perfect for a weeknight dinner or a special occasion.

**Quinoa Salad**

Ingredients:

For the Salad:

- 1 cup quinoa, rinsed
- 2 cups water or vegetable broth
- 1 cucumber, diced
- 1 bell pepper (any color), diced
- 1 cup cherry tomatoes, halved
- 1/2 cup red onion, finely chopped
- 1/4 cup Kalamata olives, sliced
- 1/4 cup feta cheese, crumbled (optional)
- Fresh herbs (such as parsley or cilantro), chopped

For the Dressing:

- 1/4 cup extra-virgin olive oil
- 2 tablespoons balsamic vinegar or red wine vinegar
- 1 teaspoon Dijon mustard
- 1 clove garlic, minced
- Salt and black pepper to taste

Instructions:

Cook Quinoa:
- In a medium saucepan, combine quinoa and water or vegetable broth. Bring to a boil, then reduce the heat to low, cover, and simmer for 15-20 minutes or until the quinoa is cooked and the liquid is absorbed. Fluff with a fork and let it cool.

Prepare Vegetables:
- In a large mixing bowl, combine the cooked and cooled quinoa with diced cucumber, diced bell pepper, cherry tomatoes, chopped red onion, Kalamata olives, and any other vegetables of your choice.

Add Feta (Optional):
- If using feta cheese, crumble it over the salad.

Make the Dressing:
- In a small bowl, whisk together extra-virgin olive oil, balsamic or red wine vinegar, Dijon mustard, minced garlic, salt, and black pepper.

Combine and Toss:
- Pour the dressing over the quinoa and vegetables. Toss everything together until well combined.

Chill (Optional):
- Refrigerate the quinoa salad for at least 30 minutes before serving to allow the flavors to meld.

Garnish with Fresh Herbs:
- Just before serving, sprinkle chopped fresh herbs (such as parsley or cilantro) over the salad.

Serve:
- Serve the quinoa salad chilled or at room temperature.

This quinoa salad is not only delicious but also packed with protein, fiber, and nutrients.

Feel free to get creative with the ingredients and adjust the dressing to your taste. It makes for a great side dish or a light and satisfying meal on its own.

**Egg Fried Rice**

Ingredients:

- 2 cups cooked and cooled jasmine rice (preferably leftover rice)
- 2 eggs, lightly beaten
- 1 cup mixed vegetables (peas, carrots, corn, and/or diced bell peppers)
- 2 green onions, finely chopped
- 2 cloves garlic, minced
- 2 tablespoons soy sauce
- 1 tablespoon oyster sauce (optional)
- 1 teaspoon sesame oil
- 2 tablespoons vegetable oil for cooking
- Salt and black pepper to taste

Instructions:

Prepare Ingredients:
- Ensure that the cooked jasmine rice is cooled and not too sticky. If using freshly cooked rice, spread it out on a tray to cool and dry a bit.
- Chop the green onions, mince the garlic, and have all other ingredients ready.

Sauté Vegetables:
- Heat vegetable oil in a large skillet or wok over medium-high heat. Add minced garlic and sauté for about 30 seconds until fragrant.
- Add mixed vegetables to the skillet and stir-fry for 2-3 minutes until they are tender but still crisp.

Push Vegetables to the Side:
- Push the vegetables to one side of the skillet, creating an empty space for the eggs.

Cook Eggs:
- Pour the beaten eggs into the empty space and let them cook for a moment. Scramble the eggs with a spatula until they are just set.

Combine with Vegetables:
- Mix the cooked eggs with the sautéed vegetables in the skillet.

Add Rice:
- Add the cooked and cooled jasmine rice to the skillet. Break up any clumps of rice and toss everything together.

Season with Sauces:
- Drizzle soy sauce and oyster sauce (if using) over the rice. Toss to combine, ensuring an even distribution of sauces.

Add Sesame Oil and Green Onions:
- Drizzle sesame oil over the rice and sprinkle chopped green onions. Toss again to incorporate the flavors.

Season and Adjust:
- Taste the egg fried rice and season with salt and black pepper as needed. Adjust the amount of soy sauce or other seasonings to your preference.

Serve:
- Serve the egg fried rice hot, garnished with additional chopped green onions if desired.

Egg fried rice is a quick and satisfying dish that you can customize by adding cooked protein like chicken, shrimp, or tofu. It's perfect for using up leftover rice and is a versatile option for a tasty meal.

**Roasted Vegetables**

Ingredients:

- Assorted vegetables, such as:
    - Bell peppers (various colors)
    - Zucchini
    - Cherry tomatoes
    - Carrots
    - Broccoli
    - Cauliflower
    - Red onion
    - Sweet potatoes
- Olive oil
- Salt and black pepper to taste
- Herbs or spices of your choice (e.g., rosemary, thyme, garlic powder, paprika)

Instructions:

Preheat the Oven:
- Preheat your oven to 425°F (220°C).

Prepare the Vegetables:
- Wash and chop the vegetables into bite-sized pieces. Ensure uniform sizing to ensure even cooking.

Toss with Olive Oil and Seasonings:
- In a large mixing bowl, toss the chopped vegetables with olive oil until they are lightly coated. Add salt, black pepper, and your choice of herbs or spices for seasoning. Mix well to ensure even distribution.

Arrange on Baking Sheet:
- Spread the seasoned vegetables in a single layer on a baking sheet. Avoid overcrowding to allow proper roasting.

Roast in the Oven:
- Place the baking sheet in the preheated oven and roast the vegetables for 20-30 minutes or until they are tender and have golden edges. Stir or toss the vegetables halfway through the cooking time for even roasting.

Check for Doneness:
- Test the doneness of the vegetables by inserting a fork or knife. They should be fork-tender with a slight caramelization on the edges.

Serve:
- Once the vegetables are roasted to your liking, remove them from the oven.
- Serve the roasted vegetables hot as a flavorful side dish.

Optional Additions:
- Add a drizzle of balsamic glaze or sprinkle grated Parmesan cheese over the roasted vegetables for additional flavor.

Roasted vegetables are incredibly versatile and can complement a variety of dishes. They make a great side for roasted or grilled meats, a topping for salads, or a delicious addition to pasta dishes. Feel free to experiment with different vegetables and seasonings to suit your taste preferences.

**Chicken Parmesan**

Ingredients:

For the Chicken Cutlets:

- 4 boneless, skinless chicken breasts
- Salt and black pepper to taste
- 1 cup all-purpose flour, for dredging
- 2 large eggs
- 2 tablespoons water
- 1 cup Italian-style breadcrumbs
- 1 cup grated Parmesan cheese
- Olive oil for frying

For Assembly:

- 2 cups marinara sauce (store-bought or homemade)
- 1 cup shredded mozzarella cheese
- 1/2 cup grated Parmesan cheese
- Fresh basil or parsley for garnish (optional)
- Cooked pasta or spaghetti for serving (optional)

Instructions:

Preheat the Oven:
- Preheat your oven to 400°F (200°C).

Prepare the Chicken Cutlets:
- Place each chicken breast between sheets of plastic wrap and pound them to an even thickness using a meat mallet. Season both sides with salt and black pepper.

Dredge in Flour:
- Set up a dredging station with three shallow bowls. Place flour in the first bowl, beaten eggs with water in the second bowl, and a mixture of breadcrumbs and grated Parmesan cheese in the third bowl.

Coat the Chicken:
- Dredge each chicken breast in the flour, shaking off excess.
- Dip the chicken into the egg mixture, allowing any excess to drip off.

- Press the chicken into the breadcrumb and Parmesan mixture, coating both sides thoroughly.

Fry the Chicken:
- Heat olive oil in a large skillet over medium-high heat. Fry the breaded chicken for 3-4 minutes per side or until golden brown and cooked through.

Drain and Pat Dry:
- Place the fried chicken on a paper towel-lined plate to drain any excess oil. Pat them dry with paper towels.

Assemble in Baking Dish:
- Spread a thin layer of marinara sauce in the bottom of a baking dish. Place the fried chicken on top of the sauce.

Top with Sauce and Cheese:
- Spoon additional marinara sauce over each chicken breast.
- Sprinkle shredded mozzarella and grated Parmesan cheese over the top.

Bake in the Oven:
- Bake in the preheated oven for 15-20 minutes or until the cheese is melted and bubbly.

Garnish and Serve:
- Garnish with fresh basil or parsley if desired.
- Serve the Chicken Parmesan hot over cooked pasta or spaghetti if you prefer.

Chicken Parmesan is a comforting and hearty dish that is sure to be a crowd-pleaser. Enjoy the combination of crispy breaded chicken, savory marinara sauce, and gooey melted cheese.

**Shrimp Scampi**

Ingredients:

- 1 pound large shrimp, peeled and deveined
- Salt and black pepper to taste
- 8 ounces linguine or spaghetti
- 3 tablespoons unsalted butter
- 3 tablespoons olive oil
- 4 cloves garlic, minced
- 1/2 teaspoon red pepper flakes (optional, for heat)
- 1/2 cup dry white wine
- Juice of 1 lemon
- Zest of 1 lemon
- 1/4 cup fresh parsley, chopped
- Grated Parmesan cheese for serving (optional)

Instructions:

Prepare the Shrimp:
- Pat the shrimp dry with paper towels and season with salt and black pepper.

Cook the Pasta:
- Cook the linguine or spaghetti according to the package instructions until al dente. Reserve about 1/2 cup of pasta cooking water before draining.

Sauté Shrimp:
- In a large skillet, heat 2 tablespoons of butter and 2 tablespoons of olive oil over medium-high heat. Add the seasoned shrimp and cook for 1-2 minutes per side until they turn pink. Remove the shrimp from the skillet and set aside.

Make the Sauce:
- In the same skillet, add the remaining 1 tablespoon of butter and 1 tablespoon of olive oil. Add minced garlic and red pepper flakes (if using). Sauté for about 1 minute until the garlic is fragrant.

Deglaze with Wine:
- Pour in the white wine, scraping up any browned bits from the bottom of the skillet. Allow the wine to simmer for 2-3 minutes to reduce.

Add Lemon and Shrimp:

- Stir in the lemon juice and lemon zest. Return the cooked shrimp to the skillet and toss to coat them in the sauce.

Combine with Pasta:
- Add the cooked pasta to the skillet and toss to combine. If needed, add some of the reserved pasta cooking water to create a silky sauce.

Finish and Garnish:
- Stir in chopped fresh parsley and season with additional salt and black pepper if needed.

Serve:
- Serve the shrimp scampi hot, optionally garnished with grated Parmesan cheese.

Shrimp scampi is a quick and delightful dish that pairs well with crusty bread or a simple green salad. Enjoy the bright and zesty flavors of this classic seafood dish!

**Caprese Panini**

Ingredients:

- 4 ciabatta rolls or slices of ciabatta bread
- 8 slices fresh mozzarella cheese
- 2 large tomatoes, thinly sliced
- Fresh basil leaves
- Balsamic glaze or balsamic reduction
- Olive oil for brushing
- Salt and black pepper to taste

Instructions:

Preheat the Panini Press or Grill Pan:
- If you have a Panini press, preheat it according to the manufacturer's instructions. If using a grill pan, heat it over medium-high heat.

Assemble the Panini:
- Cut the ciabatta rolls in half or take slices of ciabatta bread.
- On one half of each roll or slice, layer slices of fresh mozzarella, tomato, and fresh basil leaves.
- Drizzle balsamic glaze or reduction over the ingredients. Season with a pinch of salt and black pepper.

Top and Press:
- Place the other half of the rolls or slices on top to form sandwiches.
- Brush the outer sides of the sandwiches with olive oil.

Grill the Panini:
- Place the assembled sandwiches on the preheated Panini press or grill pan.
- If using a Panini press, close the lid and grill until the bread is golden brown, and the cheese is melted (about 4-6 minutes).
- If using a grill pan, press down on the sandwiches with a spatula and flip them after 2-3 minutes on each side, or until the bread is toasted, and the cheese is melted.

Serve:
- Remove the Caprese Panini from the press or grill pan.
- Optionally, drizzle more balsamic glaze over the top before serving.

Enjoy:

- Serve the Caprese Panini hot and enjoy the gooey melted mozzarella, juicy tomatoes, and fragrant basil in each bite.

Caprese Panini is a simple yet flavorful sandwich that captures the essence of the classic Caprese salad. It's perfect for a quick lunch or dinner, and the combination of fresh ingredients makes it a refreshing and satisfying choice.

**Sweet Potato Fries**

Ingredients:

- 2 large sweet potatoes, peeled and cut into matchsticks or wedges
- 2 tablespoons olive oil
- 1 teaspoon paprika
- 1 teaspoon garlic powder
- 1 teaspoon onion powder
- 1/2 teaspoon cayenne pepper (optional, for heat)
- Salt and black pepper to taste
- 2 tablespoons cornstarch (optional, for extra crispiness)
- Fresh parsley or cilantro for garnish (optional)

Instructions:

Preheat the Oven:
- Preheat your oven to 425°F (220°C).

Prepare the Sweet Potatoes:
- Peel the sweet potatoes and cut them into matchsticks or wedges, depending on your preference.

Coat with Olive Oil:
- In a large bowl, toss the sweet potato pieces with olive oil until they are well coated.

Seasoning:
- In a small bowl, mix paprika, garlic powder, onion powder, cayenne pepper (if using), salt, and black pepper.

Coat with Seasonings:
- Sprinkle the seasoning mix over the sweet potatoes and toss until evenly coated. If you want extra crispiness, you can add cornstarch and toss again.

Spread on Baking Sheet:
- Arrange the seasoned sweet potato fries in a single layer on a baking sheet. Ensure they are not crowded to allow even baking and crispiness.

Bake in the Oven:
- Bake in the preheated oven for 20-25 minutes, flipping the fries halfway through the cooking time. Bake until the sweet potatoes are golden brown and crispy.

Garnish (Optional):
- If desired, garnish the sweet potato fries with chopped fresh parsley or cilantro.

Serve:
- Serve the sweet potato fries hot as a delicious and healthier alternative to regular French fries.

Enjoy your homemade sweet potato fries as a side dish or a tasty snack. They pair well with a variety of dipping sauces such as ketchup, aioli, or yogurt-based sauces.

**Beef Stroganoff**

Ingredients:

- 1 pound (450g) beef sirloin or tenderloin, thinly sliced into strips
- Salt and black pepper to taste
- 2 tablespoons olive oil
- 1 onion, finely chopped
- 2 cloves garlic, minced
- 8 ounces (225g) mushrooms, sliced
- 2 tablespoons all-purpose flour
- 1 cup beef broth
- 2 tablespoons Worcestershire sauce
- 1 tablespoon Dijon mustard
- 1/2 cup sour cream
- Fresh parsley, chopped, for garnish
- Cooked egg noodles, rice, or mashed potatoes for serving

Instructions:

Season and Sear Beef:
- Season the beef strips with salt and black pepper. In a large skillet or pan, heat olive oil over medium-high heat. Add the beef strips and sear them quickly on all sides until browned. Remove the beef from the pan and set aside.

Sauté Onion and Garlic:
- In the same pan, add chopped onions and sauté until softened, about 2-3 minutes. Add minced garlic and cook for an additional 30 seconds.

Cook Mushrooms:
- Add sliced mushrooms to the pan and cook until they release their moisture and become golden brown.

Make the Sauce:
- Sprinkle flour over the mushroom mixture and stir well to coat. Cook for 1-2 minutes to eliminate the raw flour taste.
- Gradually pour in beef broth, Worcestershire sauce, and Dijon mustard. Stir continuously to avoid lumps and bring the mixture to a simmer.

Add Beef and Simmer:

- Return the seared beef to the pan. Allow the mixture to simmer for 5-7 minutes, allowing the flavors to meld and the sauce to thicken.

Finish with Sour Cream:
- Reduce the heat to low and stir in sour cream. Simmer for an additional 2-3 minutes, ensuring the sauce is heated through.

Adjust Seasoning:
- Taste the Beef Stroganoff and adjust the seasoning with salt and black pepper as needed.

Serve:
- Serve the Beef Stroganoff over cooked egg noodles, rice, or mashed potatoes.
- Garnish with chopped fresh parsley before serving.

Beef Stroganoff is a comforting and hearty dish that's perfect for a family dinner or a special occasion. The creamy mushroom sauce complements the tender beef, creating a flavorful and satisfying meal.

**Tomato Basil Bruschetta**

Ingredients:

- 4-5 ripe tomatoes, diced
- 1/2 cup fresh basil leaves, chopped
- 3 cloves garlic, minced
- 2 tablespoons extra-virgin olive oil
- 1 teaspoon balsamic vinegar (optional)
- Salt and black pepper to taste
- Baguette or Italian bread, sliced
- Olive oil for brushing bread

Instructions:

Prepare Tomatoes:
- Dice the ripe tomatoes and place them in a bowl.

Chop Basil:
- Chop the fresh basil leaves and add them to the bowl with tomatoes.

Add Garlic:
- Mince the garlic cloves and add them to the bowl with tomatoes and basil.

Season and Mix:
- Drizzle extra-virgin olive oil over the tomato mixture. If using balsamic vinegar, add it as well.
- Season the mixture with salt and black pepper to taste.
- Gently toss the ingredients to combine. Allow the mixture to marinate for at least 15-20 minutes to let the flavors meld.

Prepare Bread:
- Preheat your oven broiler or grill.
- Slice the baguette or Italian bread into rounds. Brush each side of the slices with olive oil.

Toast Bread:
- Place the bread slices under the broiler or on the grill for 1-2 minutes on each side, or until they are golden and crispy. Watch closely to prevent burning.

Top with Tomato Mixture:
- Remove the toasted bread from the oven or grill.
- Spoon the tomato and basil mixture generously over each slice.

Serve:
- Arrange the Tomato Basil Bruschetta on a platter and serve immediately.

This classic bruschetta is a perfect appetizer for any occasion, showcasing the vibrant flavors of fresh tomatoes and basil. It's a light and refreshing dish that's easy to prepare and always a crowd-pleaser. Enjoy!

**Chicken Fajitas**

Ingredients:

For the Chicken Marinade:

- 1.5 pounds (about 700g) boneless, skinless chicken breasts or thighs, sliced into strips
- 3 tablespoons olive oil
- 3 tablespoons lime juice
- 2 cloves garlic, minced
- 1 teaspoon ground cumin
- 1 teaspoon chili powder
- 1 teaspoon paprika
- 1/2 teaspoon dried oregano
- Salt and black pepper to taste

For the Fajita Vegetables:

- 2 bell peppers (any color), thinly sliced
- 1 large onion, thinly sliced
- 2 tablespoons olive oil
- Salt and black pepper to taste

For Serving:

- Flour or corn tortillas
- Salsa, guacamole, sour cream, shredded cheese, chopped cilantro (optional)

Instructions:

Marinate the Chicken:
- In a bowl, combine olive oil, lime juice, minced garlic, cumin, chili powder, paprika, dried oregano, salt, and black pepper. Mix well.
- Add the sliced chicken to the marinade, ensuring each piece is well coated. Cover and refrigerate for at least 30 minutes, or marinate for up to 4 hours for more flavor.

Prepare Fajita Vegetables:
- In a large skillet or pan, heat 2 tablespoons of olive oil over medium-high heat.
- Add sliced bell peppers and onions to the skillet. Sauté until the vegetables are tender-crisp and slightly caramelized. Season with salt and black pepper to taste. Transfer the vegetables to a plate and set aside.

Cook the Chicken:
- In the same skillet, add the marinated chicken strips. Cook for 5-7 minutes or until the chicken is fully cooked and has a nice sear.

Combine Chicken and Vegetables:
- Return the sautéed bell peppers and onions to the skillet with the cooked chicken. Toss everything together to combine and heat through.

Warm Tortillas:
- While the chicken and vegetables are cooking, warm the tortillas in a dry skillet or microwave.

Serve:
- Spoon the chicken and vegetable mixture onto the warmed tortillas.
- Serve with your choice of toppings such as salsa, guacamole, sour cream, shredded cheese, and chopped cilantro.

Enjoy:
- Roll up the tortillas and enjoy your homemade chicken fajitas!

Chicken fajitas are a versatile dish, and you can customize them to suit your taste.

They're perfect for a quick and delicious weeknight dinner or for entertaining friends and family.

**One-Pot Chicken and Rice**

Ingredients:

- 1.5 pounds (about 700g) bone-in, skin-on chicken thighs or drumsticks
- Salt and black pepper to taste
- 2 tablespoons olive oil
- 1 onion, finely chopped
- 2 cloves garlic, minced
- 1 cup long-grain white rice
- 1 teaspoon paprika
- 1 teaspoon dried thyme
- 1 teaspoon dried oregano
- 1 teaspoon ground cumin
- 2 cups chicken broth
- 1 cup diced tomatoes (fresh or canned)
- 1 cup frozen peas or mixed vegetables
- Fresh parsley or cilantro for garnish (optional)
- Lemon wedges for serving (optional)

Instructions:

Season Chicken:
- Season chicken thighs or drumsticks with salt and black pepper.

Sear Chicken:
- In a large, oven-safe pot or Dutch oven, heat olive oil over medium-high heat. Brown the chicken on both sides until golden brown. Remove the chicken from the pot and set it aside.

Sauté Onion and Garlic:
- In the same pot, add chopped onion and sauté until it becomes translucent. Add minced garlic and sauté for an additional 30 seconds.

Add Rice and Spices:
- Stir in the white rice, paprika, dried thyme, dried oregano, and ground cumin. Cook for 1-2 minutes, allowing the rice to toast slightly.

Pour in Liquid:
- Pour in the chicken broth, diced tomatoes (with their juice), and return the browned chicken to the pot.

Simmer:

- Bring the mixture to a simmer. Cover the pot and let it simmer on low heat for about 20-25 minutes or until the rice is cooked and the chicken is fully cooked through.

Add Vegetables:
- Add frozen peas or mixed vegetables to the pot in the last 5 minutes of cooking. Stir gently to combine.

Check for Doneness:
- Ensure the rice is tender, and the chicken reaches a safe internal temperature (165°F or 74°C).

Garnish and Serve:
- Garnish with fresh parsley or cilantro, if desired. Serve the one-pot chicken and rice hot, optionally with lemon wedges on the side.

This one-pot chicken and rice is a complete and comforting meal with minimal cleanup.

The combination of tender chicken, flavorful rice, and vegetables makes it a family-friendly dish. Enjoy!

**Broccoli Cheddar Soup**

Ingredients:

- 4 cups fresh broccoli florets (about 1 medium-sized broccoli head)
- 1 small onion, finely chopped
- 2 carrots, peeled and grated
- 2 cloves garlic, minced
- 1/4 cup unsalted butter
- 1/4 cup all-purpose flour
- 3 cups chicken or vegetable broth
- 2 cups milk (whole or 2%)
- 2 cups shredded sharp cheddar cheese
- Salt and black pepper to taste
- 1/4 teaspoon nutmeg (optional)
- Croutons or additional shredded cheddar for garnish (optional)

Instructions:

Prepare Broccoli:
- Cut the broccoli into small florets. Peel and chop the broccoli stalks into smaller pieces.

Sauté Vegetables:
- In a large pot, melt the butter over medium heat. Add chopped onions, grated carrots, and minced garlic. Sauté until the vegetables are softened.

Make Roux:
- Sprinkle flour over the sautéed vegetables and stir continuously to make a roux. Cook for 2-3 minutes to eliminate the raw flour taste.

Add Broth and Milk:
- Gradually whisk in the chicken or vegetable broth and milk, ensuring there are no lumps. Bring the mixture to a simmer and cook for about 10 minutes, or until it thickens slightly.

Add Broccoli:
- Add the chopped broccoli florets and stalks to the pot. Simmer for an additional 10-15 minutes or until the broccoli is tender.

Blend (Optional):
- For a smoother texture, use an immersion blender to blend part of the soup, leaving some broccoli pieces intact. Alternatively, transfer a portion

of the soup to a blender and blend until smooth before returning it to the pot.

Add Cheddar Cheese:
- Stir in the shredded cheddar cheese until it is melted and well combined with the soup.

Season:
- Season the soup with salt, black pepper, and nutmeg (if using). Adjust the seasoning according to your taste.

Serve:
- Ladle the Broccoli Cheddar Soup into bowls. Garnish with croutons or additional shredded cheddar cheese if desired.

Enjoy:
- Serve the soup hot and enjoy the comforting flavors of broccoli and cheddar.

Broccoli Cheddar Soup is a cozy and satisfying dish, perfect for warming up on chilly days. Serve it as a starter or pair it with a crusty bread for a complete and hearty meal.

**Margherita Flatbread**

Ingredients:

- 1 pre-made flatbread or naan bread
- 2 medium-sized tomatoes, thinly sliced
- 1 cup fresh mozzarella cheese, sliced or torn
- Fresh basil leaves
- 2 tablespoons olive oil
- Salt and black pepper to taste
- Balsamic glaze (optional, for drizzling)

Instructions:

Preheat the Oven:
- Preheat your oven to 425°F (220°C).

Prepare Flatbread:
- Place the flatbread on a baking sheet or pizza stone.

Assemble the Flatbread:
- Drizzle olive oil over the flatbread, spreading it evenly to the edges.
- Arrange the thinly sliced tomatoes and fresh mozzarella over the flatbread.
- Season with salt and black pepper to taste.

Bake in the Oven:
- Place the assembled flatbread in the preheated oven and bake for 10-12 minutes or until the crust is golden and the cheese is melted and bubbly.

Add Fresh Basil:
- Once out of the oven, scatter fresh basil leaves over the hot flatbread.

Drizzle with Balsamic Glaze (Optional):
- For an extra touch of flavor, drizzle balsamic glaze over the top of the Margherita flatbread.

Slice and Serve:
- Slice the flatbread into wedges or squares and serve immediately.

Margherita flatbread is a quick and delicious option for a light lunch, dinner, or appetizer.

The combination of fresh tomatoes, mozzarella, and basil creates a burst of flavors reminiscent of the classic Margherita pizza. Enjoy!

**Creamy Garlic Mashed Potatoes**

Ingredients:

- 2 pounds (about 1 kg) russet potatoes, peeled and cut into chunks
- 4 cloves garlic, peeled
- 1/2 cup unsalted butter, softened
- 1/2 cup heavy cream or whole milk
- Salt and black pepper to taste
- Chopped fresh chives or parsley for garnish (optional)

Instructions:

Boil Potatoes and Garlic:
- Place the peeled and chopped potatoes and whole garlic cloves in a large pot. Cover with cold water and add a pinch of salt. Bring to a boil over medium-high heat and cook until the potatoes are fork-tender.

Drain:
- Drain the cooked potatoes and garlic in a colander.

Mash Potatoes:
- Return the drained potatoes and garlic to the pot or a large mixing bowl. Mash them using a potato masher or a fork until smooth.

Add Butter:
- Add the softened butter to the mashed potatoes and garlic. Mix well until the butter is fully incorporated.

Add Cream/Milk:
- Pour in the heavy cream or whole milk. Continue to mash and mix until the potatoes reach your desired consistency. Add more cream/milk if needed.

Season:
- Season the mashed potatoes with salt and black pepper to taste. Adjust the seasoning according to your preference.

Whip for Creaminess (Optional):
- For an extra creamy texture, you can use an electric mixer or a hand mixer to whip the mashed potatoes for a few minutes.

Garnish and Serve:
- Transfer the creamy garlic mashed potatoes to a serving bowl. Garnish with chopped fresh chives or parsley if desired.

Enjoy:

- Serve the mashed potatoes hot as a side dish to complement your main course.

Creamy garlic mashed potatoes are a crowd-pleaser and a perfect accompaniment to roasted meats, grilled chicken, or any dish that pairs well with mashed potatoes. The addition of garlic brings a delicious savory flavor to the classic side dish.

**Pesto Pasta**

Ingredients:

- 8 ounces (about 225g) pasta (such as spaghetti, linguine, or your favorite type)
- 2 cups fresh basil leaves, packed
- 1/2 cup grated Parmesan cheese
- 1/2 cup pine nuts (or walnuts)
- 2 cloves garlic, peeled
- 1/2 cup extra-virgin olive oil
- Salt and black pepper to taste
- Optional: 1/2 cup grated Pecorino Romano cheese
- Optional: Cherry tomatoes, halved, for garnish
- Optional: Fresh basil leaves for garnish

Instructions:

Cook the Pasta:
- Cook the pasta according to the package instructions in a large pot of salted boiling water until al dente. Reserve about 1/2 cup of pasta cooking water and then drain the pasta.

Prepare Pesto Sauce:
- In a food processor, combine fresh basil, grated Parmesan cheese, pine nuts, and peeled garlic cloves. Pulse until the ingredients are finely chopped.

Add Olive Oil:
- With the food processor running, slowly pour in the extra-virgin olive oil in a steady stream until the mixture becomes a smooth sauce. If needed, scrape down the sides of the food processor with a spatula.

Season:
- Season the pesto sauce with salt and black pepper to taste. Adjust the seasoning according to your preference.

Combine with Pasta:
- In a large mixing bowl, toss the cooked and drained pasta with the prepared pesto sauce. If the sauce is too thick, you can add a bit of the reserved pasta cooking water to reach your desired consistency.

Optional Additions:

- If desired, mix in grated Pecorino Romano cheese for an extra layer of flavor.

Garnish:
- Garnish the pesto pasta with halved cherry tomatoes and fresh basil leaves if you like.

Serve:
- Serve the pesto pasta immediately, either warm or at room temperature.

Pesto pasta is a quick and delicious meal that celebrates the fresh flavors of basil. Feel free to customize it by adding grilled chicken, cherry tomatoes, or extra cheese. It's a versatile dish that's perfect for a simple weeknight dinner or a delightful lunch.

## Honey Garlic Glazed Salmon

Ingredients:

- 4 salmon fillets (about 6 ounces each), skin-on or skinless
- Salt and black pepper to taste
- 3 tablespoons honey
- 2 tablespoons soy sauce
- 2 tablespoons olive oil
- 3 cloves garlic, minced
- 1 tablespoon fresh ginger, grated (optional)
- Sesame seeds and chopped green onions for garnish (optional)

Instructions:

Preheat the Oven:
- Preheat your oven to 400°F (200°C).

Season the Salmon:
- Pat the salmon fillets dry with paper towels. Season both sides with salt and black pepper.

Make the Honey Garlic Glaze:
- In a small bowl, whisk together honey, soy sauce, minced garlic, and grated ginger (if using).

Sear the Salmon:
- In an oven-safe skillet, heat olive oil over medium-high heat. Once hot, add the salmon fillets, skin-side down if applicable. Sear for 2-3 minutes until the salmon has a golden crust.

Brush with Glaze:
- Brush the tops of the salmon fillets with the honey garlic glaze.

Transfer to Oven:
- Transfer the skillet to the preheated oven and bake for 8-10 minutes, or until the salmon is cooked through and flakes easily with a fork. Baste the salmon with more glaze halfway through the baking time.

Broil (Optional):
- If you want a caramelized finish, you can switch the oven to broil for the last 1-2 minutes of cooking. Keep a close eye to prevent burning.

Garnish:
- Remove the salmon from the oven and brush with additional glaze. Sprinkle sesame seeds and chopped green onions for garnish if desired.

Serve:
- Serve the honey garlic glazed salmon hot, over rice or with your favorite side dishes.

This honey garlic glazed salmon is a perfect combination of sweet and savory flavors. The glaze caramelizes in the oven, creating a glossy and delicious coating for the salmon. It's a quick and impressive dish that's great for both weeknight dinners and special occasions.

**Avocado Toast**

Ingredients:

- 2 slices of your favorite bread (sourdough, whole grain, or multigrain)
- 1 ripe avocado
- Salt and black pepper to taste
- Optional toppings: poached or fried egg, cherry tomatoes, red pepper flakes, feta cheese, sesame seeds, or fresh herbs

Instructions:

Toast the Bread:
- Toast the slices of bread to your desired level of crispiness.

Prepare the Avocado:
- While the bread is toasting, cut the ripe avocado in half, remove the pit, and scoop the flesh into a bowl.

Mash the Avocado:
- Mash the avocado with a fork until you reach your desired level of smoothness. Some people prefer a chunkier texture, while others like it smoother.

Season:
- Season the mashed avocado with salt and black pepper to taste. You can also add a squeeze of fresh lemon or lime juice for extra brightness.

Spread on Toast:
- Once the bread is toasted, spread the mashed avocado evenly over each slice.

Optional Toppings:
- Get creative with toppings! Some popular options include a poached or fried egg, sliced cherry tomatoes, a sprinkle of red pepper flakes, crumbled feta cheese, sesame seeds, or fresh herbs like cilantro or parsley.

Serve:
- Serve the avocado toast immediately while the bread is still warm.

Avocado toast is not only delicious but also highly customizable. Feel free to experiment with different toppings and seasonings to suit your taste. It's a nutritious and satisfying breakfast or snack that's quick to prepare and always a crowd-pleaser.

**Lemon Herb Roasted Potatoes**

Ingredients:

- 2 pounds (about 1 kg) baby potatoes, washed and halved
- 3 tablespoons olive oil
- 2 tablespoons fresh lemon juice
- 2 cloves garlic, minced
- 1 teaspoon dried rosemary
- 1 teaspoon dried thyme
- 1 teaspoon dried oregano
- Salt and black pepper to taste
- Zest of one lemon
- Fresh parsley, chopped, for garnish (optional)

Instructions:

Preheat the Oven:
- Preheat your oven to 400°F (200°C).

Prepare the Potatoes:
- Wash the baby potatoes and cut them in half. If the potatoes are larger, you can quarter them for even cooking.

Make the Marinade:
- In a bowl, whisk together olive oil, fresh lemon juice, minced garlic, dried rosemary, dried thyme, dried oregano, salt, and black pepper.

Coat the Potatoes:
- Toss the halved potatoes in the lemon herb marinade, ensuring they are well coated.

Arrange on Baking Sheet:
- Spread the potatoes in a single layer on a baking sheet lined with parchment paper or lightly greased.

Roast in the Oven:
- Roast the potatoes in the preheated oven for 30-35 minutes or until they are golden brown and crispy on the edges. You can toss them halfway through the cooking time for even browning.

Add Lemon Zest:
- Once the potatoes are out of the oven, sprinkle the zest of one lemon over them. The lemon zest adds a burst of fresh flavor.

Garnish and Serve:
- Garnish the lemon herb roasted potatoes with chopped fresh parsley if desired.

Serve Hot:
- Serve the potatoes hot as a flavorful side dish.

These lemon herb roasted potatoes are a delicious and aromatic addition to your meals. The combination of lemon and herbs adds brightness and depth of flavor, making them a perfect accompaniment to a variety of dishes.

**Chicken Caesar Wraps**

Ingredients:

For the Caesar Dressing:

- 1/2 cup mayonnaise
- 2 tablespoons grated Parmesan cheese
- 1 tablespoon Dijon mustard
- 2 teaspoons anchovy paste (optional)
- 1 clove garlic, minced
- 1 tablespoon lemon juice
- Salt and black pepper to taste

For the Chicken:

- 1 pound (about 450g) boneless, skinless chicken breasts
- Salt and black pepper to taste
- 1 tablespoon olive oil
- 1 teaspoon garlic powder
- 1 teaspoon dried oregano
- 1 teaspoon dried thyme

For the Wraps:

- Flour tortillas or wraps
- Romaine lettuce, chopped
- Cherry tomatoes, halved
- Grated Parmesan cheese
- Optional: Croutons for crunch

Instructions:

Prepare the Caesar Dressing:
- In a bowl, whisk together mayonnaise, grated Parmesan cheese, Dijon mustard, anchovy paste (if using), minced garlic, lemon juice, salt, and

black pepper. Adjust the seasoning to your taste. Refrigerate the dressing until ready to use.

Cook the Chicken:
- Season the chicken breasts with salt, black pepper, garlic powder, dried oregano, and dried thyme.
- In a skillet over medium-high heat, heat olive oil. Add the seasoned chicken breasts and cook for 6-8 minutes per side or until the internal temperature reaches 165°F (74°C). Let the chicken rest for a few minutes before slicing it into strips.

Assemble the Wraps:
- Lay out the flour tortillas or wraps on a flat surface.
- Spread a generous spoonful of Caesar dressing onto each tortilla.

Add Chicken and Toppings:
- Place slices of cooked chicken in the center of each tortilla.
- Add chopped Romaine lettuce, halved cherry tomatoes, and grated Parmesan cheese on top of the chicken.

Optional Crunch:
- For an extra crunch, you can add croutons to the wraps.

Fold and Serve:
- Fold the sides of each tortilla inward and then roll it up from the bottom to create a wrap.

Serve:
- Serve the Chicken Caesar wraps immediately. You can cut them in half for easier handling.

These Chicken Caesar wraps are a delicious and convenient way to enjoy the classic Caesar salad with the added protein of grilled chicken. They make a perfect lunch or dinner option and are great for a quick and satisfying meal.

**Ratatouille**

Ingredients:

- 1 large eggplant, diced
- 2 medium zucchinis, sliced
- 1 large bell pepper, diced (use a mix of colors for visual appeal)
- 4 ripe tomatoes, diced
- 1 large onion, thinly sliced
- 4 cloves garlic, minced
- 2 tablespoons tomato paste
- 2 tablespoons olive oil
- 1 teaspoon dried thyme
- 1 teaspoon dried rosemary
- 1 teaspoon dried oregano
- Salt and black pepper to taste
- Fresh basil or parsley for garnish

Instructions:

Prepare the Vegetables:
- Dice the eggplant, slice the zucchinis, dice the bell pepper, dice the tomatoes, and thinly slice the onion.

Cook the Onion and Garlic:
- In a large, oven-safe skillet or casserole dish, heat olive oil over medium heat. Add the thinly sliced onion and minced garlic. Sauté until the onion becomes translucent.

Add Tomato Paste:
- Stir in the tomato paste and cook for an additional 2-3 minutes, allowing it to caramelize slightly.

Layer Vegetables:
- Add the diced eggplant, sliced zucchinis, diced bell pepper, and diced tomatoes to the skillet. Arrange them in an overlapping spiral or concentric circles for a visually appealing presentation.

Season:
- Sprinkle dried thyme, dried rosemary, dried oregano, salt, and black pepper over the vegetables.

Bake:

- Preheat your oven to 375°F (190°C). Transfer the skillet to the preheated oven and bake for 45-55 minutes or until the vegetables are tender and the flavors meld together.

Garnish:
- Once out of the oven, garnish the ratatouille with fresh basil or parsley.

Serve:
- Serve the ratatouille as a side dish or over cooked quinoa, rice, or pasta.

Ratatouille is a versatile dish that can be served hot, warm, or at room temperature. It's a celebration of seasonal vegetables and is both delicious and visually impressive. Enjoy this classic French dish as a main course or a flavorful side dish.

**Stuffed Bell Peppers**

Ingredients:

- 4 large bell peppers (any color)
- 1 cup cooked rice (white or brown)
- 1 pound (about 450g) ground beef or turkey
- 1 onion, finely chopped
- 2 cloves garlic, minced
- 1 can (14 ounces) diced tomatoes, drained
- 1 cup black beans, drained and rinsed
- 1 cup corn kernels (fresh, frozen, or canned)
- 1 teaspoon chili powder
- 1 teaspoon ground cumin
- 1/2 teaspoon paprika
- Salt and black pepper to taste
- 1 cup shredded cheese (cheddar, Monterey Jack, or a blend)
- Fresh cilantro or parsley for garnish (optional)
- Salsa, sour cream, or guacamole for serving (optional)

Instructions:

Preheat the Oven:
- Preheat your oven to 375°F (190°C).

Prepare the Bell Peppers:
- Cut the tops off the bell peppers, remove the seeds and membranes, and lightly brush the outside with olive oil. Place the bell peppers in a baking dish.

Cook the Meat:
- In a skillet over medium heat, cook the ground beef or turkey until browned. Drain any excess fat.

Sauté Onion and Garlic:
- Add chopped onion to the skillet and sauté until it becomes translucent. Add minced garlic and cook for an additional 1-2 minutes.

Mix Ingredients:
- In a large mixing bowl, combine the cooked meat and onion mixture with cooked rice, diced tomatoes, black beans, corn, chili powder, ground cumin, paprika, salt, and black pepper. Mix well.

Stuff the Peppers:
- Stuff each bell pepper with the mixture, pressing it down gently.

Top with Cheese:
- Sprinkle shredded cheese over the top of each stuffed pepper.

Bake:
- Cover the baking dish with foil and bake in the preheated oven for 25-30 minutes, or until the peppers are tender.

Broil (Optional):
- If you want a golden-brown cheese crust, uncover the peppers and broil for an additional 2-3 minutes until the cheese is bubbly and lightly browned.

Garnish and Serve:
- Garnish with fresh cilantro or parsley if desired. Serve the stuffed bell peppers hot, with salsa, sour cream, or guacamole on the side.

These stuffed bell peppers make for a wholesome and satisfying meal. You can customize the filling based on your preferences, adding ingredients like quinoa, beans, or different spices. Enjoy the combination of savory meat, vegetables, and cheesy goodness in each bite!

**Creamy Spinach Artichoke Dip**

Ingredients:

- 1 cup frozen chopped spinach, thawed and drained
- 1 can (14 ounces) artichoke hearts, drained and chopped
- 1/2 cup mayonnaise
- 1/2 cup sour cream
- 1 cup shredded mozzarella cheese
- 1/2 cup grated Parmesan cheese
- 1 teaspoon minced garlic
- 1/2 teaspoon onion powder
- 1/4 teaspoon dried oregano
- 1/4 teaspoon dried basil
- Salt and black pepper to taste
- 1 cup cream cheese, softened
- Optional: Crushed red pepper flakes for a hint of heat
- Optional: Extra shredded cheese for topping

Instructions:

Preheat the Oven:
- Preheat your oven to 375°F (190°C).

Prepare Spinach and Artichokes:
- Thaw the frozen chopped spinach and drain any excess liquid. Chop the drained artichoke hearts.

Mix Ingredients:
- In a large mixing bowl, combine the chopped spinach, chopped artichokes, mayonnaise, sour cream, shredded mozzarella, grated Parmesan, minced garlic, onion powder, dried oregano, dried basil, salt, black pepper, and softened cream cheese. Mix well until all ingredients are evenly combined.

Add Optional Ingredients:
- If you like a bit of heat, you can add crushed red pepper flakes to the mixture.

Transfer to Baking Dish:
- Transfer the mixture to a baking dish, spreading it evenly.

Optional Cheese Topping:
- Sprinkle extra shredded cheese on top if you desire an extra cheesy crust.

Bake:

- Bake in the preheated oven for 25-30 minutes or until the dip is hot and bubbly, and the top is golden brown.

Serve:
- Remove from the oven and let it cool slightly before serving.

Enjoy:
- Serve the creamy spinach artichoke dip with tortilla chips, bread slices, or vegetable sticks.

This creamy spinach artichoke dip is a crowd-pleaser and can be enjoyed as a warm and comforting appetizer. The combination of creamy cheese, spinach, and artichokes creates a delicious and flavorful dip that's sure to be a hit at any gathering.

**Lemon Butter Tilapia**

Ingredients:

- 4 tilapia fillets
- Salt and black pepper to taste
- 1/2 cup all-purpose flour, for dredging
- 2 tablespoons olive oil
- 4 tablespoons unsalted butter
- 3 cloves garlic, minced
- 1/4 cup chicken or vegetable broth
- Juice of 1 lemon (about 2-3 tablespoons)
- Zest of 1 lemon
- 2 tablespoons chopped fresh parsley
- Lemon slices for garnish (optional)

Instructions:

Season and Dredge Tilapia:
- Season tilapia fillets with salt and black pepper. Dredge each fillet in flour, shaking off excess.

Cook Tilapia:
- In a large skillet, heat olive oil over medium-high heat. Add the tilapia fillets and cook for about 2-3 minutes per side, or until golden brown and cooked through. Remove the tilapia from the skillet and set aside.

Make Lemon Butter Sauce:
- In the same skillet, add 2 tablespoons of butter and minced garlic. Sauté the garlic for about 1 minute until fragrant.

Deglaze with Broth:
- Pour in the chicken or vegetable broth to deglaze the skillet, scraping up any browned bits from the bottom.

Add Lemon Juice and Zest:
- Add the lemon juice and lemon zest to the skillet. Stir to combine.

Finish the Sauce:
- Reduce the heat to low, and add the remaining 2 tablespoons of butter to the skillet. Stir until the butter is melted and the sauce is smooth.

Return Tilapia to Skillet:

- Return the cooked tilapia fillets to the skillet, coating them in the lemon butter sauce. Cook for an additional 1-2 minutes to heat the fish through.

Garnish:
- Sprinkle chopped fresh parsley over the tilapia. Garnish with lemon slices if desired.

Serve:
- Serve the lemon butter tilapia hot, spooning extra sauce over the fillets.

This lemon butter tilapia is a quick and elegant dish that brings out the natural flavors of the fish with a citrusy and buttery kick. It pairs well with rice, quinoa, or a side of steamed vegetables for a light and delicious meal.

**Sausage and Peppers**

Ingredients:

- 1 pound (about 450g) Italian sausage links (sweet or hot)
- 2 tablespoons olive oil
- 1 large onion, thinly sliced
- 3 bell peppers (a mix of red, green, and yellow), thinly sliced
- 3 cloves garlic, minced
- 1 can (14 ounces) crushed tomatoes
- 1 teaspoon dried oregano
- 1 teaspoon dried basil
- Salt and black pepper to taste
- Red pepper flakes (optional, for added heat)
- Fresh basil or parsley for garnish (optional)
- Rolls, pasta, or rice for serving

Instructions:

Brown the Sausages:
- In a large skillet, heat olive oil over medium-high heat. Add the Italian sausage links and brown them on all sides. This should take about 5-7 minutes. Remove the sausages from the skillet and set them aside.

Sauté Onions and Peppers:
- In the same skillet, add sliced onions and bell peppers. Sauté over medium heat until the vegetables are softened and slightly caramelized, about 8-10 minutes.

Add Garlic:
- Add minced garlic to the skillet and sauté for an additional 1-2 minutes until fragrant.

Combine with Crushed Tomatoes:
- Pour in the crushed tomatoes and add dried oregano, dried basil, salt, black pepper, and red pepper flakes (if using). Stir to combine.

Simmer:
- Return the browned sausages to the skillet, nestling them into the sauce. Cover the skillet and let it simmer over medium-low heat for about 20-25 minutes, allowing the flavors to meld.

Check for Doneness:

- Check the sausages for doneness by ensuring they reach an internal temperature of 160°F (71°C).

Garnish and Serve:
- Garnish with fresh basil or parsley if desired. Serve the sausage and peppers hot over rolls, pasta, or rice.

Sausage and peppers are a versatile dish that can be enjoyed in various ways. Whether you serve it on a roll for a sandwich, over pasta, or alongside rice, it's a comforting and flavorful meal that's perfect for family dinners or casual gatherings.

**Chicken Noodle Soup**

Ingredients:

- 1 tablespoon olive oil
- 1 onion, diced
- 2 carrots, sliced
- 2 celery stalks, sliced
- 3 cloves garlic, minced
- 1 teaspoon dried thyme
- 1 teaspoon dried rosemary
- 8 cups chicken broth
- 1 bay leaf
- 2 boneless, skinless chicken breasts
- 2 cups egg noodles
- Salt and black pepper to taste
- Fresh parsley, chopped, for garnish (optional)
- Lemon wedges for serving (optional)

Instructions:

Sauté Vegetables:
- In a large pot, heat olive oil over medium heat. Add diced onions, sliced carrots, and sliced celery. Sauté until the vegetables are softened, about 5-7 minutes.

Add Garlic and Herbs:
- Add minced garlic, dried thyme, and dried rosemary to the pot. Sauté for an additional 1-2 minutes until the garlic is fragrant.

Pour in Chicken Broth:
- Pour in the chicken broth and add a bay leaf. Bring the broth to a simmer.

Add Chicken:
- Add the boneless, skinless chicken breasts to the simmering broth. Let them cook for about 15-20 minutes or until they are cooked through.

Remove Chicken and Shred:
- Remove the cooked chicken breasts from the pot and shred them using two forks. Return the shredded chicken to the pot.

Cook Noodles:

- Add egg noodles to the pot and cook according to the package instructions until they are al dente.

Season:
- Season the soup with salt and black pepper to taste. Adjust the seasoning as needed.

Garnish and Serve:
- Garnish the chicken noodle soup with chopped fresh parsley if desired. Serve hot with lemon wedges on the side for a citrusy kick.

Enjoy:
- Ladle the comforting chicken noodle soup into bowls and enjoy the warmth and nourishment.

This homemade chicken noodle soup is not only delicious but also customizable. Feel free to add additional vegetables like peas or spinach, and adjust the seasonings according to your preference. It's a timeless recipe that brings warmth and comfort with every spoonful.

**BBQ Pulled Pork Sandwiches**

Ingredients:

For the Pulled Pork:

- 3-4 pounds pork shoulder or pork butt
- Salt and black pepper to taste
- 1 tablespoon olive oil
- 1 large onion, sliced
- 4 cloves garlic, minced
- 1 cup chicken or vegetable broth
- 1 cup barbecue sauce (plus extra for serving)
- 1 tablespoon brown sugar
- 1 tablespoon Dijon mustard
- 1 tablespoon Worcestershire sauce

For the Sandwiches:

- Hamburger buns or sandwich rolls
- Coleslaw (optional, for topping)

Instructions:

Preheat the Oven:
- Preheat your oven to 325°F (163°C).

Season and Sear the Pork:
- Season the pork shoulder or pork butt with salt and black pepper. In a large oven-safe pot or Dutch oven, heat olive oil over medium-high heat. Sear the pork on all sides until browned.

Sauté Onions and Garlic:
- Add sliced onions and minced garlic to the pot. Sauté until the onions are softened.

Create Braising Liquid:
- Pour in chicken or vegetable broth, barbecue sauce, brown sugar, Dijon mustard, and Worcestershire sauce. Stir to combine.

Braise the Pork:

- Place the seared pork back into the pot, ensuring it's partially submerged in the braising liquid. Cover the pot with a lid.

Slow Cook in Oven:
- Transfer the pot to the preheated oven and slow cook for 3-4 hours, or until the pork is fork-tender and easily pulls apart.

Shred the Pork:
- Once the pork is cooked, remove it from the pot and shred it using two forks. Discard any excess fat.

Simmer in Sauce:
- Strain the braising liquid and return the shredded pork and strained liquid to the pot. Simmer for an additional 10-15 minutes until the pork is well-coated and the sauce thickens slightly.

Assemble the Sandwiches:
- Toast the hamburger buns or sandwich rolls. Spoon the pulled pork onto the bottom half of each bun.

Optional Toppings:
- Top the pulled pork with extra barbecue sauce and coleslaw if desired.

Serve:
- Place the top half of the bun over the pulled pork, creating a sandwich. Serve the BBQ pulled pork sandwiches hot.

These BBQ pulled pork sandwiches are perfect for a crowd-pleasing meal, whether it's a casual dinner or a barbecue gathering. The tender and flavorful pulled pork pairs wonderfully with the sweetness and tanginess of the barbecue sauce. Add coleslaw for a refreshing crunch, and you have a delicious and satisfying sandwich.

**Chocolate Chip Cookies**

Ingredients:

- 1 cup (2 sticks) unsalted butter, softened
- 3/4 cup granulated sugar
- 3/4 cup packed brown sugar
- 2 large eggs
- 1 teaspoon vanilla extract
- 2 1/4 cups all-purpose flour
- 1 teaspoon baking soda
- 1/2 teaspoon salt
- 2 cups semisweet chocolate chips

Instructions:

Preheat the Oven:
- Preheat your oven to 375°F (190°C). Line baking sheets with parchment paper.

Cream Butter and Sugars:
- In a large mixing bowl, cream together the softened butter, granulated sugar, and brown sugar until light and fluffy.

Add Eggs and Vanilla:
- Beat in the eggs one at a time, ensuring each is fully incorporated. Add the vanilla extract and mix well.

Combine Dry Ingredients:
- In a separate bowl, whisk together the flour, baking soda, and salt.

Combine Wet and Dry Ingredients:
- Gradually add the dry ingredients to the wet ingredients, mixing just until combined. Be careful not to overmix.

Fold in Chocolate Chips:
- Gently fold in the chocolate chips until evenly distributed throughout the cookie dough.

Scoop Dough onto Baking Sheets:
- Using a cookie scoop or spoon, drop rounded tablespoons of dough onto the prepared baking sheets, leaving enough space between each cookie.

Bake:

- Bake in the preheated oven for 9-11 minutes, or until the edges are golden but the centers are still soft. Keep in mind that the cookies will continue to set as they cool.

Cool on Baking Sheet:
- Allow the cookies to cool on the baking sheets for a few minutes before transferring them to a wire rack to cool completely.

Enjoy:
- Once cooled, enjoy your homemade chocolate chip cookies with a glass of milk or your favorite beverage!

Feel free to customize the recipe by adding nuts, using different types of chocolate chips, or experimenting with a sprinkle of sea salt on top before baking. These chocolate chip cookies are a timeless treat that's sure to bring joy to anyone who enjoys a classic and delicious dessert.

www.ingramcontent.com/pod-product-compliance
Lightning Source LLC
LaVergne TN
LVHW081602060526
838201LV00054B/2027